HOW TO WIN

Lawrence James

Contents

"Think of life as a raffle – you can't win if you don't buy a ticket."

INTRODUCTION

When growing up, I saw life from a lot of perspectives there is a quote, it says: "Don't measure your life by how many breaths you take, but by what takes your breath away." there are a lot of things and experience that takes your blood, your sweat and all your efforts but it will not yield a good result quickly, some things will make you go through a difficult time, when I finished my college I started thinking about the way to survive as a teen trying to build the future, when I was at the University I saw some students being at University and working two jobs to make ends meet, and it occurred to me and I noticed that they were doing things that takes their breath away and waxing their strength away. That quote inspired me to make some pretty big changes in my life, which led me on a path that I'm incredibly happy to be on. People have asked me whether I feel that I am "winning" at life or not. I suppose that some people might think so, while others would balk at choices I’ve made, and where I’ve ended up. Personally, I feel that the idea of “winning” at life implies that we’re competing with others, rather than following our own unique, individual journeys. There are several actions people can take in order to attain various levels of personal success and fulfillment. We'll be taking look into a lot of steps that can help to attain winning at different levels of life.

POINT 1
Growing as a Person

Practice thinking confident thoughts. Confidence, like many things, is a skill that can be learned. Even if you don't start off feeling confident, the more you practice, the better you'll get and the happier you'll feel. Think positively about your life. When faced with an obstacle, tell yourself that you can overcome it.

Even if you’re not feeling confident, try acting confident with body language. Stand up straight while you're walking or sitting. Avoid standing with your arms crossed. Instead, put your hands on your hips.

Just smiling, even if you force it, can help you feel instantly happier and more confident, as your brain releases endorphins.

Embrace positive thinking, it's normal to have self-doubts, but you can overcome them. Every time you start having negative thoughts about yourself, stop yourself and re-frame the thought into a positive or neutral one. For example, if you find yourself thinking "I am so worthless," think instead, "I am really valuable to myself and others."

POINT 2

Never stop learning

Learning never end they say. Never stop educating yourself throughout your life. It will keep your brain sharp, and give you interesting things to discuss with other people. Start with subjects that are interesting to you, such as video game design or historical costuming, politics, science and others.

Be eager to learn every day, try to learn something new every day, read a book or meet new people or do something different. Because when it comes to winning, having more knowledge is basically power.

Educate yourself about what is happening in the world, advances in science, medicine, politics, art, and current events. This keeps you in touch with what is going on.

Try to learn a new skill, such as knitting, speaking a foreign language, or understanding astrophysics.

Reading books and articles, watching the news and documentaries, or doing online tutorials are all great ways to keep learning.

Whether you're honing your skills or diving into a new subject that interests you, you'll find that constantly learning new things keeps your mind sharp and your senses agile. People can be absolute masters at their craft, but new techniques, materials, and ideas keep evolving on a daily basis. When we stop learning, we stagnate. And worse than that, we can get arrogant and stuck in our own ways. Someone might have gained wealth and accolades by doing something a particular way for decades, but what if they could do better, more easily, by changing one little technique? As an added bonus, learning new things – especially new languages!–helps to create fresh, new pathways in your brain. According to health experts they said learning new things can help someone to be safe from mental deterioration conditions or issue like

Alzheimer and dementia. Don't only learn new things, learn how to try, if you find that you have an opportunity to grow, learn, or explore something new, but you’re afraid to try it because it’s different or scary, see if you have the courage to do it anyway. You’ll undoubtedly learn a lot by trying, and at least you won’t spend the rest of your life wondering what would have happened if you’d taken the chance.

Think of life as a raffle – you can't win if you don't buy a ticket.

POINT 3
Learn from your mistakes

No matter how successful you are, no matter how healthy you are, no matter what you do or don't do, you're going to make mistakes and experience failure. Sometimes these incidents will be your fault, sometimes they won't. It's how you respond to them that will determine your ability to be successful at life.

Your attitude toward life shapes how you experience

things. Let go of your expectations and accept life as it is. This will empower you to handle whatever comes your way.

Don't be afraid to make mistakes. When you do make a mistake, ask yourself how did things go wrong, what did you learn from it and what will you do differently next time?

To learn from your mistakes, you must first take accountability for them. Acknowledge where you went wrong so that you can fix it. Accept the consequences of your actions. Remember that life is a series of choices. To take control of your life, you need to take responsibility for those choices, rather than acting as if everything happens to you. Instead of blaming someone else, accept responsibility, and do what you need to do to fix the situation.

Make the choice to not react to things in a negative or destructive way. For example, if your friend said something mean about you behind your back, don't get try to get revenge or snap at them. Instead, ignore the comment or politely confront them.

While you cannot always control what happens to you in life, you can control how you react to it. For example, if you get diagnosed with a disease, instead of saying "why me?" learn how to live the life you've always wanted.

POINT 4
Build confidence/Passion

Step out of your comfort zone in order to build confidence. Have you heard the phrase "a comfort zone is a beautiful place, but nothing ever grows there"? It may sound a bit trite, but it's actually very true. Comfort zones are soothing and cozy, but they can also allow us to stagnate and grow complacent. People need new situations to challenge them, because it's only through overcoming challenges that we can really grow. If you've ever tended a garden, you'll know that plants need a bit of stress in order to truly thrive. Too much stress will harm or even kill them (much like humans), but just a little bit, just enough, encourages stronger growth and more abundant yields.

Although it can be a little nerve-racking at first, these experiences will help you gain confidence and the resources to deal with the uncertainties of life. You might try something as intense as skydiving or rock-climbing or something more mundane like meeting new people or speaking in front of a crowd.

Take small steps to get better. If you have social anxiety, for example, your small step could be talking to one unknown person a week or making 1 phone call per week. You can eventually work up to going to an event by yourself or dealing with people on a regular basis.

Try to do something that pushes you each day. Even small shifts can end up making a big difference in your life.

Build your passion, how many people do you know who are slogging through careers and jobs they can't stand so that hopefully, one day, they can finally retire and then do the things that they enjoy? Does that sound fulfilling to you?

Life is short, and far too many people spend most of their time enduring existence rather than enjoying it. When you make a career out of something you love, you pour sincere effort into it because it's actually important to you.

I’d call that a win, wouldn’t you?

Your passion defines you, your passion is what you have great calling for and what you can't do without, it can be in form of a vocation, in form of a skill, music or art, use your passion and interests to find a fulfilling vocation. Your vocation is your calling in life that gives you meaning. Sometimes, this is your profession, but it can also be a hobby, a passion, or a side project. Study your interests, passions, and hobbies. Use your passion to guide you towards a vocation that is meaningful to you.

Think about your values—what really lights you up and gets you excited? What do you want to be remembered for? Then, try to figure out what you can do that aligns with that. Your passion can help you to impact and improve lives.

If your job isn't your passion in life, try to think of all the positive benefits of it. Make a list of all the good things about your job, such as having things you like, making a difference in people's lives, or making enough money to buy a house.

Don't feel like you necessarily have to make big changes all at once. You can still incorporate your passion into your daily life. For instance, if you love acting, you might not be able to quit your job and move to Hollywood, but you might find that you enjoy acting in a local community theater. Do what you love and what makes you happy. Be passionate in everything you do. When you show and excrete passion through actions

POINT 5

Embrace gratitude

Express gratitude on a daily basis. Gratitude lets you lead a life where you feel content and fulfilled. Once a day, find something that you are grateful for. Write it down or say how much it means to you.

Being grateful affirms that there are good things in life, even if not everything is good at the moment. For example, if a loved one has died, you have every right to be sad. Instead of focusing on their death, however, focus on how grateful you were to have them in your life.

Keep a gratitude journal. Jot down all the little things that happened throughout each day that you were grateful for. This will create a habitual practice of gratitude.

Try to see good in everything, now, this doesn't mean to be an insufferable optimist all the time. Things go to hell now and then, and being in denial about crappy situations doesn't do anyone any good. It's important to recognize when you're dealing with an "ugh" situation, rather than trying to polish it up and insist that it's fine, really, everything's fine, hahahah – that's toxic positivity. When unpleasant situations arise, acknowledge them, work through them the best you can, and try to see the upside if there is one.

Practice mindfulness. The practice of mindfulness helps you experience each sensation and detail in the moment. Take a few minutes to notice everything around you. Pay attention to the sights, sounds, feel, and smells. Don't assign value judgments to things (such as a "beautiful sky" or "cold wind"), but simply notice them.

Meditation is a great way to get started with mindfulness. For 15 minutes each day sit quietly somewhere. Breathe deeply, and focus only on your breath. If you get distracted, return your attention to your breath.

You can also practice mindfulness while eating. Notice what you're eating: the texture (smooth, crunchy, chewy), the taste (is it salty? Is it sweet? Is it spicy?), the temperature (hot, cold). Try avoiding distractions, such as TV or reading, while you eat.

Mindfulness can help with depression and anxiety, reduce your stress, boost your memory, increase your focus, and create better emotional stability.

POINT 6

Cultivate Self-Discipline

No matter what it is you do, be disciplined and dedicated about it. Do what needs to be done in order to achieve your goals, and hold yourself to a high standard of behavior to make it happen. If your health is a priority, create a solid exercise schedule and personal diet plan, and stick to them. Do you want to improve your education? Set aside X amount of time per day to work on a course or program that you've enrolled in. When you're occupied with your studies, act as though nothing else in the world exists. Think about some people you look up to and who you would say have won at life. Consider their stories and journeys. What you'll find is they worked hard and stayed disciplined to achieve what they did.

POINT 7

Care more for yourself

The impression people give about you might be right and might be wrong at times. When those impression seems to be your weakness try to work yourself and fix things out. But often you don't have to care about what people say because their thoughts about you might not be the real version of you. Too many people end up on paths that don’t fulfill them, simply because they’re pushed to do so by others, or they feel that they “should” do certain things because they’re expected. Some often focus on what people tell them to do because they don't have plans for themselves.

You can’t win at life if it’s not your life that you’re living. You just have to desist from that, stop living that fake life. Choose to live wisely.

Don’t get trapped in other people’s thoughts and expectations, even if they’re your parents or partners, friends, family members and others. Everyone has their own path to walk, and you're not going to put sincere effort into a path that you feel forced to be on; you'll be a lot happier and more successful in your endeavors.

POINT 8

Plan for the ways to achieve your goals

Example, if your goal is to buy a car make a set of steps and goals that can help you save enough for your down payment by a same date.

If you'd like to learn something new, then make a schedule for yourself to practice for some hours per week, on specific projects.

By doing so, you have a way to measure your progress and

document your achievements. These small, realistic goals are invaluable for keeping you motivated.

And how will you know when you win at life if you don't know what winning looks like to you – goals can help you with that.

POINT 9
Learn To Adapt

There is a saying that goes something like: “If you want to make God laugh, tell him/her your plans.” Life is known to change at the drop of a hat, and that can cause people a lot of stress, drama, and even trauma. After all, when we expect things to unfold a certain way and then they don’t, or something arises that throws our tidy little world into chaos, we can fall apart a little bit.

The key is to remain flexible enough to adapt to any circumstance.

Strive for goals, but be ready to change direction as needed – basically like taking a different route to your end destination.

Don't get too attached to specific outcomes, but try to appreciate the journey, and the learning that happens while you're getting there.

Acknowledge that every single situation is an opportunity for personal awareness and growth, and there's often something to be grateful for.

If you want to win, sometimes you have to look for the win in your current situation.

POINT 10

External Stress

This may sound like a no-brainer, but a lot of people make their lives a lot more difficult than necessary by not eliminating unnecessary stressors. Sometimes, the contributing factor to one's stress can be a person who consistently drains your energy.

Additional factors can be annoying neighbors, unneeded drains on your finances, other people's expectations of you, and moderate commitments that you really aren't feeling.

Try to eliminate whatever isn't needed, and simplify your life as much as possible.>Distance yourself from emotional vampires. Move out of the city if you're being constantly assaulted by sirens, sounds, and smells that stress you out and overwhelm you. Cancel your entertainment subscriptions if you're not taking full advantage of them.

Basically, trim out everything that doesn't bring you joy, or don't fulfill you.

If winning at life means walking a path that you find fulfilling, it's far easier to do that when you're not weighed down by unnecessary burdens.

Live practically, but don't deny yourself. Some people believe that in order to be successful, they need to be miserly. Basically, saving every penny, or only spending on things that are absolutely necessary.

While being practical in terms of spending choices is a good idea, it's also important to enjoy your life.

Investing in an adult-sized bouncy castle for your backyard might not be a wise investment, but clothes that you love, delicious food, and trips that inspire you can bring an extraordinary amount of joy into your world.

Try not to spend money that you don't have, as nobody likes to contend with the crippling interest on credit card debt. Set aside a bit of money from every payment you get, and put those funds towards things that make you smile. Invest in yourself, and in the things that make you happy. After all, this beautiful life was meant to be enjoyed, right?

Everyone's going to have their own idea of what "winning" at life looks like. Each individual has their own priorities, life goals, and concepts of what success means. For one person, winning will mean living in opulent wealth, with expensive clothes and cars and whatnot.

To another person, success might mean a quiet, simple life

of peaceful self-sufficiency in a mountain cabin.

Regardless of what your own concept of winning might be, there are always opportunities for growth and personal development.

Never mind what other people's priorities and wants are. Try not to compare yourself to others, but determine what happiness and success mean to you. After all, you can't win at someone else's life; you can only win at yours.

Hopefully some of these tips can help too

Set up specific goals, you need to know where you are going. Imagine you are in a race, but you don't know where the finishing line is, would you be able to win? No, you wouldn't. That's why you need a specific target, you need to know exactly what direction are you going in, and where the finishing line is. And learn to work towards something rather than working aimlessly.

You need to learn to take responsibility for your actions

You can't blame others for your mistakes, and you can't use excuses. Winners are people that are self-aware about their own mistakes; they understand that it's their choices and decisions that brought them there. Winners don't use excuses, they find solutions.

Form a winning habit

Strange right? But that's what you have to do. You have to

form a winning habit, and habits are hard to develop. To form a winning habit, you need to start looking things at a different perspective; you have to look at them as challenges. You should try to challenge yourself daily, form a habit of doing every day something you couldn't do before.

"Winning is a habit, become a winner in life," *Vince* Lo*mbardi* quote

Don’t be afraid to fail

You shouldn’t be afraid to fail, what you should do is learn to accept your failures as a lesson. You shouldn’t let failing demotivate you, you should get the best out if it, and that’s the lesson and you should use that lesson as a guide to help you win next time.

Take risks

Don’t be afraid of taking a risk. Because if you are too cautious, you might miss the opportunity and you might not have a second one.

Stay focused

Keeping your focus towards the finishing line is what matters. Don't slack, always keep your mind and focus on your goal. Because if you are not focused, then you are not doing things seriously! And if you are not doing things seriously you can't become a winner, guys. It's simple!

Be committed

The main difference between losers and winners is that

winners are committed to winning. Winners know what they want and therefore do whatever they have to do, to get there. You need to stay dedicated in order to become a winner in life.

You have to be willing to work harder than others

And in the end, it all comes to working hard. Let me give you an example with sports – If your competition is doing 100 push-ups every day, you have to do 200. Don’t forget that the more effort you put in, the better results you will have, and that’s not only in sports, it applies to all fields of life.

CONCLUSION

Lastly create dream, vision: if you dream then you can do it. Many people think that if they try something and it does not work right away, it means it will never work. If you keep trying, however, you may succeed.

Don't be afraid of yourself. Have confidence and don't be self-conscious.

Being a winner in life really just means learning how to grow as a person while creating healthy, happy relationships. The best way to do this is to create a fulfilling lifestyle filled with love and positivity. Make sure to cultivate healthy thoughts, relationships, and practices in your daily life.

www.ingramcontent.com/pod-product-compliance
Lightning Source LLC
LaVergne TN
LVHW050346160826
845677LV00014B/3820

* 9 7 9 8 3 5 9 8 6 2 1 5 8 *